ACTION

BEATING THE IMPOSTOR SYNDROME

IDEAS INTO ACTION SERIES
Aimed at managers and executives who are concerned with their own and others' development, each book in this series gives specific advice on how to complete a developmental task or solve a leadership problem.

LEAD CONTRIBUTORS
Portia Mount and Susan Tardanico

SPECIAL CONTRIBUTOR
Rie Ingold

CONTRIBUTOR
Sophia Zhao

DIRECTOR OF ASSESSMENTS, TOOLS, AND PUBLICATIONS
Sylvester Taylor

MANAGER, PUBLICATION DEVELOPMENT
Peter Scisco

EDITOR
Stephen Rush

ASSOCIATE EDITOR
Shaun Martin

DESIGN, LAYOUT, AND COVER DESIGN
Ed Morgan, navybluedesign.com

RIGHTS AND PERMISSIONS
Kelly Lombardino

CCL No. 001002

ISBN No. 978-1-60491-529-7

Center for Creative Leadership
www.ccl.org

IDEAS
INTO
ACTION

BEATING THE IMPOSTOR SYNDROME

Portia Mount
Susan Tardanico

Center for
Creative
Leadership

IDEAS INTO ACTION SERIES

This series of books draws on the practical knowledge that the Center for Creative Leadership (CCL) has generated since its inception in 1970. The purpose of the series is to provide leaders with specific advice on how to complete a developmental task or solve a leadership challenge. CCL's researchers and educators work together to understand and generate practical responses to the ever-changing circumstances of leadership and organizational challenges. Our proven and cutting edge ideas serve leaders and organizations around the world, who put those ideas into action every day. We believe you will find the Ideas Into Action series of books an important addition to your leadership toolkit.

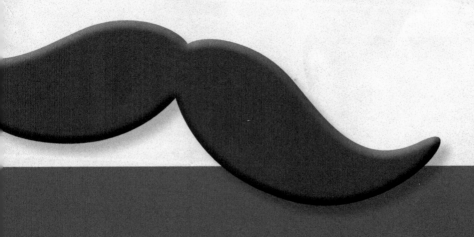

CONTENTS

In Brief

The Impostor Syndrome is a well-researched, well-documented phenomenon that occurs when successful and intelligent professionals feel they do not deserve their accomplishments and that they have faked their way to success. This syndrome can cause negative stress, fear, anxiety, loss of confidence, and can eventually lead to derailment. However, by overcoming inaccurate beliefs about yourself and your abilities, you can overcome the Impostor Syndrome and enjoy a more fulfilling career.

First, you should focus on the facts of your success, and document what skills and techniques you possess helped you achieve those successes. Next, you should identify and challenge your limiting beliefs. These beliefs may hold you back from really owning your accomplishments, because they give you an inaccurate picture of what success actually looks like. Then, you should get clear on the strengths you possess, instead of just focusing on your weaknesses, and take the time to maximize and showcase those strengths. Finally, you should talk to others to help obtain a clearer picture of your skills and your accomplishments. Additional perspectives can help you see the flaws in your own perspective, and give you the information you need in order to accurately view yourself as competent.

By completing these four steps, you can overcome the debilitating nature of the Impostor Syndrome, and truly embrace your accomplishments and abilities.

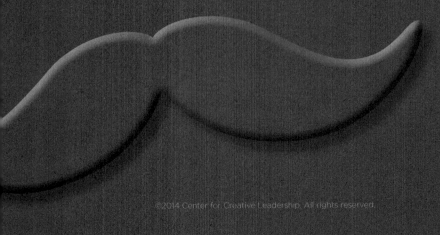

Are **YOU** an **IMPOSTOR**?

Career experts and mental health professionals call it the "Impostor Syndrome." Successful and intelligent leaders who have earned promotions, accolades, and recognition from their bosses, their peers, and their teams feel, deep down, like frauds. They worry that it's only a matter of time before they are found out and their colleagues question their abilities.

Leaders who exhibit the Impostor Syndrome share many traits. They are typically ambitious, high-achieving individuals who believe they have not earned success. They frequently discount their own accomplishments. Negative stress, anxiety, and fear remind these leaders of their sense of inadequacy.

Does this sound like you or someone you know?

This book explains the developmental challenges that arise when "impostors" fail to recognize their abilities and are unable to internalize their accomplishments. After reading this book, you will learn how to recognize and manage the symptoms of the Impostor Syndrome to create a productive and fulfilling career.

War Games

Charlie, a retired US army colonel, served for seven years in key strategic leadership roles at the Pentagon. After hearing the authors speak about the Impostor Syndrome at a conference in Washington, DC, Charlie approached the dais full of emotion. "All these years, I had no idea what it was," he said. "I thought I was broken. I used to sit behind a desk, wearing this decorated uniform, feeling like a scared, incompetent nine-year-old in a hero's costume. For the life of me, I couldn't understand why they kept promoting me."

How IMPOSTOR SYNDROME Affects YOU

Leaders who exhibit the Impostor Syndrome have an intense fear of failure, a lack of confidence, and anxiety. These feelings often manifest as procrastination, risk aversion, and workaholism. Imagined impostors are also reluctant to ask questions for fear of appearing unintelligent. Such constraints negatively affect job performance and satisfaction for leaders at all levels, from individual contributors to members of an organization's executive team.

Furthermore, negative and self-defeating thoughts can keep even the most highly respected leaders from developing their skills and talents. These missed career opportunities diminish contributions for those leaders, their teams, their organizations, and their communities.

The Impostor Syndrome can also lead to overwhelming negative stress, which plays out in a number of ways, such as sleeplessness and a weakened immune system. Additionally, the intense fear and stress experienced by imagined impostors create blurred work-life boundaries because those affected feel they must work 24/7 to keep their faux incompetence from being exposed. They believe there is no choice: work must take precedence over all else.

How IMPOSTOR SYNDROME Affects OTHERS

Let's begin with an example of the impact of the Impostor Syndrome on the people you lead. Clare is the executive vice president of a large, successful company and has nine direct reports. In a recent culture survey conducted by the company, her direct reports described their working environment as "disempowering," "demotivating," and "lacking in trust." These descriptors were so dramatically different from the results of other corporate functions that Clare's organization brought in consultants to help Clare and her peers figure out what was going on.

Despite her outstanding credentials and obvious intelligence, experience, and magnetic personality, Clare feels like a pretender. She feels unworthy of her position, which affects her ability to make decisions. As a result, Clare keeps her team in perpetual "analysis paralysis." She asks for more and more data, test cases, and proof of potential outcomes—and

then fails to make decisions. Additionally, because Clare doesn't trust her worth as a leader and decision maker, she projects distrust onto her reports, which results in her rarely delegating work to others. Clare's team doesn't understand her behavior, and her direct reports think they've done something to lose her trust. "I keep playing back different situations, wondering what I did to make her lose faith in me," one says. "Where did I go wrong?"

The unfortunate part of this story is that Clare genuinely cares about her people. She was deeply concerned when she saw the results of the culture survey and devastated when she received some of this feedback. However, breaking free of the Impostor Syndrome is hard work. "I care so much about them that I don't want to make a mistake or a bad decision that will affect them or the function," Clare says.

Blowback: How the Impostor Syndrome Affects Your Team

If you suffer from the Impostor Syndrome, your deep sense of unworthiness drives behaviors that can negatively impact others. Just as Clare's drive to micromanage and to make the "right" decisions negatively affect her team, your actions could be hurting your team in similar ways. For example:

If you're driven to . . .	The result might be that . . .
micromanage	your people feel untrusted, incapable, and paranoid.
make decisions slowly	your people feel demotivated because they can't make progress.
be perfect	your people feel insecure because nothing they do is good enough.
worry excessively	your people lose confidence because you lack confidence.
exhibit workaholism	your people feel that they're expected to work the same hours, and they become overworked and stressed.

Wait! I Can Explain!

The insidious, unrelenting sense of inadequacy that plagues some leaders often remains masked. As such, people with the Impostor Syndrome frequently rationalize their success in the following ways:

"I got lucky."

"I was in the right place at the right time."

"I just work harder than everyone else."

"It's just because they like me."

"Anyone could have done it."

"I had a lot of help/connections."

"Someone must have made a mistake."

"I fooled them . . . again."

It's important that you not confuse the Impostor Syndrome with humility. Displaying modesty about your abilities is much different from believing you lack certain strengths or that you have somehow faked your way into your current position. Being humble can be a positive trait, and it might be expected in your organization or as part of your cultural heritage. Feeling like an impostor is a negative belief that handicaps your performance, and you should address it.

However, leaders who exhibit the Impostor Syndrome can go beyond rationalizations. They often make extraordinary efforts to cover up their supposed inadequacy and to avoid being found out. Many leaders work hard, but sufferers of the Impostor Syndrome take an obsessive, nearly frantic approach to every detail. The coping and protection mechanisms that kick in for sufferers of the Impostor Syndrome include

overpreparing

"Even when I know my material, I overprepare because I worry about looking foolish or incompetent."

"I tend to be a perfectionist and have a hard time letting go of the details."

"It's not uncommon for me to work more than 10 hours a day."

"I tend to assign equal weight to every task—everything is high-stakes."

holding back talents and opinions

"I avoid situations where I think I might fail or where I'm not 100 percent sure I know what I'm doing."

"It's hard for me to ask for help, even when I really need it."

"I frequently feel scared that I might fail, even when I'm familiar with the task."

maintaining a low profile

"I find it difficult to accept compliments and praise."

"I have a hard time advocating for myself to get raises and promotions."

"I avoid situations that call attention to me; I prefer to be in the background."

procrastination

"I wait until the last minute to work on important projects."

not finishing

"I hold off launching anything new until I'm sure everything is in place."

self-sabotage

"When I experience a setback or failure, I have a hard time bouncing back."

"I am very critical about my personal appearance."

"It's easier for me to remember the failures in my career than the successes."

"I often feel anxious and worried that I'm not doing a good job, even if there is evidence to the contrary."

Do any of these actions sound familiar?

If so, you may be suffering from the Impostor Syndrome. However, you can overcome the Impostor Syndrome by reassessing your abilities and applying some simple strategies.

Stand Out and Speak Up

Irene was always an overachiever. As the youngest of five girls in her family, she felt that she needed to work harder than any of the other kids to stand out. After graduation, she went into pharmaceutical marketing, was promoted very quickly, and eventually was made head of a multimillion-dollar account.

This account was incredibly demanding, and Irene worked diligently to exceed expectations. Although she never felt like she was doing a good enough job, the account grew substantially under her leadership, becoming one of her firm's most profitable clients. Irene received praise from both her supervisor and the executive leadership. Despite all of this, she finds it hard to ask for a promotion or for more money because she doesn't feel like she has earned it. She sees less qualified people moving ahead of her, and she knows it's because she has such a hard time advocating for herself.

Overcoming the Impostor Syndrome

Flawed beliefs about success, failure, and self-worth lie at the root of the Impostor Syndrome. To overcome this debilitating mode of thinking, you need to become aware of inaccurate beliefs that you hold and realign what you believe about yourself and what you experience, observe, and do. These four steps can help:

- focus on facts

- challenge your limiting beliefs

- get clear on your strengths

- talk about it

Let's look more closely at these actions by using a successful CEO with an enviable track record as an example. We will call him Steve.

Steve's peers, employees, and customers see him as a smart, intuitive person and respect his views and his actions. Born and raised in Brooklyn by parents of very little means, he was determined to make a better life for himself. Steve attended a local college, obtained a job, rose through the ranks at two public companies, and then started his own company. Five years later, a major financial services company acquired his company, and Steve worked his way up to become CEO of the entire enterprise.

During his stint as CEO, Steve began working with an executive coach. It quickly became evident in their work together that not only was Steve unable to acknowledge his leadership strengths, but he also believed he needed to change who he was to deserve his position. Steve's feelings of inadequacy stemmed, in part, from his belief that financial means and a pedigreed education equated to intelligent, effective leaders.

He diminished every career success he'd had, saying he was just lucky and that he had people who helped him along the way.

He also believed his Brooklyn accent and distinctive style of communicating was not CEO-like, despite feedback from colleagues and other stakeholders that they loved his refreshingly direct and honest style. In order for Steve to overcome his feelings of inadequacy, his executive coach directed Steve to assess his own skills and performance through a new lens by taking four steps.

Step 1 | Focus on Facts

Dumb Luck

People who suffer from the Impostor Syndrome often pass off their successes to "dumb luck." Smart people put themselves in a position to get lucky. And once the "lucky break" takes place, the diligent, resourceful, strategic person capitalizes on it.

Steve's track record of success (double-digit growth during a recession, high employee engagement, and impressive financial returns) belies his internal limiting beliefs. He sees the world around him through a distorted lens. If asked to explain how he achieved such impressive success, Steve's stock response is "I'm lucky, and I work harder than everyone else." Luck and doing whatever it takes may play a part in his success, but Steve needed to see that all of his success can't be tied to those factors alone. Therefore, the executive coach had Steve conduct a personal success inventory to make the facts about his career visible so that he could focus on them.

Using the Personal Success Inventory worksheet, Steve listed dozens of his major successes and identified the core skills he drew on to achieve them. Steve pressed himself to honestly assess how much of each success was attributable to luck versus specific skills, strategies, and execution. His reflection and analysis showed him that the stories he was telling himself and others about his successes were more myth than reality. Like Steve, you can take steps to separate fact from fiction about your success by completing the following worksheet.

Personal Success Inventory

Do you **own** your success? Use this worksheet to examine your accomplishments and determine how much of your success was actually due to something other than luck. By conducting an objective assessment of your achievements, you are likely to see a pattern that suggests you applied new skills, approaches, or insights that allowed you to accomplish those goals.

Directions: Complete this worksheet with as many successes as possible. At a minimum, include at least five successes from the past one to three years. The more successes you can list over a longer timeframe, the more insight you can achieve!

If you (or your coach) feel you are unable to objectively conduct this assessment alone, you might want to get a more balanced perspective by soliciting input from colleagues who worked with you on these projects. You may also want to complete a 360-degree feedback assessment in order to gain a clearer picture of your successes.

List your accomplishments in chronological order.

Personal Success Inventory

Challenge or Assignment	Date	Accomplishment	Success Drivers: Skills/Capabilities/ Personal Qualities That Helped You Succeed
Taking lead position for important client	May 2013	Increased business 30%	Sales, negotiation, listening, commitment to the customer

Personal Success Inventory

Challenge or Assignment	Date	Accomplishment	Success Drivers: Skills/Capabilities/Personal Qualities That Helped You Succeed

After completing your inventory list, take some time to analyze it and mine for deeper insights. Here are some questions to get you started:

- **Observe the chronology of your successes.** Did one achievement lead you to another? What specific skills, capabilities, and attributes did you develop through each experience that added to your overall competence?

- **From the list, pick your three proudest accomplishments and describe three specific things you did to achieve each goal.** The more detailed your description, the better. Write your description in a very objective and straightforward way, as if you're a newspaper reporter. Be careful not to discount anything because it was "too easy" or "something anyone could have done."

- **In cases where you listed a high percentage of success due to other team members, list what you did to lead the team to success.** How did you facilitate the achievement of the goal through other people?

- **Refer to your sheet and pick one recent challenge you overcame.** What did it look like when you successfully dealt with this challenge? What did you learn about yourself in the process? What specific moments stand out, and how can you replicate them or transfer the lessons you learned to another challenge you face?

Once you've thoughtfully answered these questions, step back and consider whether you have truly owned your successes and whether you've acknowledged the facts about your achievements. Having a strong self-awareness of your strengths and successes is the first step to overcoming the Impostor Syndrome.

Step 2 | Challenge Your Limiting Beliefs

Steve believed that his experiences and personality traits were unable to justify his success. After all, successful CEOs have advanced degrees from Ivy League schools, speak with perfect diction and a proper accent, are always poised, and if they had pulled themselves up by their own Herculean efforts, show little or no sign of their hardscrabble roots or modest heritage. This set of limiting beliefs kept Steve in denial about his ability and legitimacy to be a successful CEO.

Steve's coach gave him an assignment: identify top-performing CEOs who had attended lesser-known colleges or who hadn't earned a degree at all. In addition, Steve's coach assigned him to identify several highly successful, respected CEOs who spoke with distinctive regional accents that might be considered outside the norm. As he researched, Steve began to see that his assumptions about CEO success factors were flawed. In fact, he learned that many CEOs he admired had actually overcome similar challenges in life or had some of the same qualities that he had discounted as "not CEO-like."

When Steve brought the results of his assignment to his next coaching session, his coach used them to explain that attributes such as the ability to earn stakeholder trust, to communicate and inspire vision, and to make quality decisions (all of which were among Steve's strengths) are far more accurate indicators of effective leadership than those attributes Steve believed were most important.

Steve learned that where leaders attended school, what their early financial conditions were, and what accent they used were largely irrelevant to leadership success.

It's vital to acknowledge and embrace your capabilities and skills if you suffer from the Impostor Syndrome. A solid awareness of the external facts can often challenge the powerful and limiting beliefs you hold.

See the complete
worksheet at the
end of the book.

worksheet

Breaking Through Your Limited Beliefs

Like Steve, it's time for you to break through your limiting beliefs.
Complete these three steps.

Identify Your Beliefs about Success

Steve thought that successful CEOs needed to have Ivy League degrees, speak with perfect diction and a proper accent, and come from stable, comfortable backgrounds. What are your beliefs about what you need to do, be, or have in order to succeed?

Breaking Through Your Limited Beliefs

In order for me to succeed (in my current role or my ultimate goal), I need to **do**, **be**, or **have** the following:

DO	BE	HAVE

Because of the following limitations,
I believe I am not worthy of my current position or success:

I have not done...	I am not...	I do not have...

Go on a Fact Hunt

Consider that your perceived success criteria may not, in fact, be accurate. Do some research and find facts and examples of others with similar attributes (or perceived limitations) who have achieved success in your field. Document these examples.

Reassess Your Beliefs

Armed with the facts, consider that your own limiting beliefs may be your greatest barrier to success. What if these limitations aren't limitations at all, or not as significant as you've assumed they are? Which of your current beliefs may be holding you back?

Step 3 | Get Clear On Your Strengths

When Steve's coach asked him what his strengths were, Steve fumbled a bit and eventually said, "I work harder than anyone else." When pressed for more, he said, "I guess people like working with and for me." Then, he launched into all the ways he needs to improve to be even more effective in his role, primarily focusing on how to improve his weaknesses.

The coach handed Steve a blank piece of paper and instructed him to write down 20 things he did well. At first, Steve looked like a deer in the headlights, so the coach brainstormed with him to get started. Then, the coach gave Steve five minutes to list his 20 items. This time-bound exercise helped Steve ignore the inner critic that would debate and discount each item before it made it to the page.

For the next two coaching sessions, Steve and his coach went through his list of strengths and talked about how each of them played out in the workplace. They brainstormed how he can use them in even more meaningful ways. By talking in concrete terms about his strengths, Steve came to see that they were real, were valuable, and helped define his leadership.

People who suffer from the Impostor Syndrome often overlook their strengths and instead focus on their weaknesses.

After all, they're convinced of their incompetence, so what better way to reinforce that belief than to focus on shortcomings? However, research shows many weaknesses occur because leaders are unaware of their strengths. For instance, a leader who believes he or she lacks management skills may try micromanaging to compensate, which creates a whole host of problems. Once this leader sees that he or she does possess good management skills, this can lessen the desire to micromanage, and thus awareness of a strength helps to alleviate a weakness. You can begin to shift your thinking by conducting a strengths inventory and then dedicating time to showcasing and maximizing those strengths.

worksheet

See the complete worksheet at the end of the book.

Strengths Inventory

Set an alarm for five minutes and **write down 10 things you do well** (e.g., creating strategy, developing others, thinking analytically, leading teams). If you're having trouble getting started, consider asking a trusted friend or colleague to help you brainstorm.

Strengths Inventory

10 Things I do well.

1.
2.
3.
4.
5.
6.
7.
8.
9.
10.

Reflect on the List You Just Developed

What do you notice about the things you've listed? Are there any common factors or skill sets?

Reflecting on what you do well, what did you have to do to develop those strengths?

How do these strengths play out in your day-to-day job? What could you do to further use your strengths to the benefit of your team or organization?

What can you do to counteract the inner critic that perpetuates negative or self-defeating thoughts? Write down three ideas.

If you showed this list to others, what else would they add to it? Consider showing this list to a trusted colleague, friend, or mentor in order to receive his or her feedback.

Step 4 | Talk About It

The most competent people are good at leveraging the strengths and expertise of others. Asking for help is not a sign of weakness. It is a sign of wisdom.

It's difficult for sufferers of the Impostor Syndrome to share their feelings of inadequacy with others.

After all, they are afraid of being found out!

Why would they risk exposure and increase their vulnerability? But as with so many emotional and psychological burdens, sharing your feelings and thoughts with someone you trust can greatly reduce stress and strain.

At first, Steve resisted this fourth step, saying that there was no one in his organization he could trust with this kind of information. What if he planted seeds of doubt in those he was leading? Steve's coach encouraged him to reach out to another CEO, Dave, with whom Steve had forged a relationship during CCL's Leadership at the Peak program for C-Suite executives. Steve and Dave had agreed to serve as mentors and sounding boards for each other, but Steve had never taken Dave up on it, feeling like his challenges were probably trivial when compared to Dave's.

Finally, Steve made the call, and the ensuing conversation was the capstone of Steve's journey in overcoming the Impostor Syndrome. As it turned out, Dave had many of the same thoughts and feelings. Steve was amazed. Dave was an incredibly strong, confident, and successful CEO—how could he be a victim of the Impostor Syndrome? This exchange helped Steve see the folly of his own beliefs, and he and Dave agreed to keep the lines of communication open, serving as confidantes for one another.

Sufferers of the Impostor Syndrome are often shocked to find that people close to them—people they respect—have the very same feelings. This revelation often helps them realize the flaws in their own self-perception. How could someone who is so successful, so talented, and so strong possibly feel this way? It's crazy! Yes, it is. Sharing with others is the first step toward building a support system that will not only relieve you of your false beliefs but enhance your performance as a leader.

Who can you talk to? Obviously, the answer to this question differs depending on your unique situation. Here are some potential avenues to pursue:

- **a peer in another function at your organization/company**

- **an established mentor**

- **a peer outside your organization/company who understands the pressures you are under**

- **an executive coach**

- **a former boss or colleague from another company**

- **bloggers and authors who have published on the Impostor Syndrome and have avenues for online chats and community building among imagined impostors**

Parting Thoughts

Rachel Sams, writing in the *Baltimore Business Journal*, says that experts believe as many as 70 percent of people feel like impostors at least once in their lives. Impostor Syndrome takes an exacting toll and could be holding you back or compromising your talents, impact, and career trajectory.

There is hope.

You can manage and overcome the Impostor Syndrome by utilizing the following behaviors:

- **focus on facts**

- **challenge your limiting beliefs**

- **get clear on your strengths**

- **talk about it**

It takes emotional honesty, introspection, and feedback from others to achieve the self-awareness and self-acceptance needed to combat the Impostor Syndrome. But the time and energy invested produces substantial dividends in terms of health, outlook, and performance. After reading this book, ask yourself if you've become adept at explaining away or minimizing evidence of your success and never truly owning your accomplishments. If you have, you may live in fear of being unmasked. Take heart. The Impostor Syndrome is a well-researched, well-documented phenomenon. You are not alone. With acceptance, self-awareness, and support, you can utilize the skills and talents you already possess to benefit others, strengthen your organization, and achieve your own leadership goals.

Background

This book is based on CCL's work in helping leaders recognize and embrace their own strengths as a means of fostering leadership development, as discussed in Robert E. Kaplan's work *Internalizing Strengths* (1999). Kaplan's work found that helping executives see their own strengths and talents, as opposed to just helping them correct their deficits and weaknesses, is an essential part of the development experience. CCL has also conducted research into helping leaders see the value of ethical self-promotion, and has published books aimed at helping leaders utilize self-promotion as a means of furthering their leadership development: *Selling Yourself without Selling Out: A Leader's Guide to Ethical Self-Promotion* (2006), and *The Truth about Sucking Up: How Authentic Self-Promotion Benefits You and Your Organization* (2009).

Suggested Resources

Clance, P. R. (1985). *The impostor phenomenon: Overcoming the fear that haunts your success.* Atlanta, GA: Peachtree Publishers.

Harvey, J. C., Katz, C. (1985). *If I'm so successful, why do I feel like a fake? The impostor phenomenon.* New York: St. Martin's Press.

Hernez-Broome, G., McLaughlin, C., Trovas, S. (2006). *Selling yourself without selling out: A leader's guide to ethical self-promotion.* Greensboro, NC: Center for Creative Leadership.

Hernez-Broome, G., McLaughlin, C., Trovas, S. (2009). *The truth about sucking up: How authentic self-promotion benefits you and your organization.* Greensboro, NC: Center for Creative Leadership.

Kaplan, R. E. (1999). *Internalizing strengths: An overlooked way of overcoming weaknesses in managers.* Greensboro, NC: Center for Creative Leadership.

Laursen, L. (2008, February 15). No, you're not an impostor. *Science.* http://dx.doi.org/10.1126/science.caredit.a0800025

Sams, R. (2008, June 19th). Are you an impostor? Phenomenon makes executives doubt their own abilities, skills. *Baltimore Business Journal.* http://www.bizjournals.com/baltimore/stories/2008/06/23/smallb1.html?page=all. Retrieved January 3, 2013.

Young, V. (2011). *The secret thoughts of successful women.* New York: Crown Business.

Notes

Breaking Through Your Limited Beliefs

In order for me to succeed (in my current role or my ultimate goal),
I need to **do**, **be**, or **have** the following:

DO	BE	HAVE

Because of the following limitations,
I believe I am not **worthy of** my current position or success:

I have not done...	I am not...	I do not have...

Breaking Through Your Limited Beliefs

Go on a Fact Hunt

Consider that your perceived success criteria may not, in fact, be accurate. Do some research and find facts and examples of others with similar attributes (or perceived limitations) who have achieved success in your field. Document these examples.

_____

_____

_____

_____

_____

_____

_____

Reassess Your Beliefs

Armed with the facts, consider that your own limiting beliefs may be your greatest barrier to success. What if these limitations aren't limitations at all, or not as significant as you've assumed they are? Which of your current beliefs may be holding you back?

_____

_____

_____

_____

_____

_____

_____

Strengths Inventory

10 Things I do well.

1.

2.

3.

4.

5.

6.

7.

8.

9.

10.

Strengths Inventory

Reflect on the List You Just Developed

What do you notice about the things you've listed? Are there any common factors or skill sets?

_____

_____

_____

_____

Reflecting on what you do well, what did you have to do to develop those strengths?

_____

_____

_____

How do these strengths play out in your day-to-day job? What could you do to further use your strengths to the benefit of your team or organization?

_____

_____

_____

What can you do to counteract the inner critic that perpetuates negative or self-defeating thoughts? Write down three ideas.

_____

_____

_____

If you showed this list to others, what else would they add to it? Consider showing this list to a trusted colleague, friend, or mentor in order to receive his or her feedback.

_____

_____

_____

About the Center for Creative Leadership

The Center for Creative Leadership (CCL) is a top-ranked, global provider of leadership development. By leveraging the power of leadership to drive results that matter most to clients, CCL transforms individual leaders, teams, organizations, and society. Our array of cutting-edge solutions is steeped in extensive research and experience gained from working with hundreds of thousands of leaders at all levels. Ranked among the world's Top 5 providers of executive education by *Financial Times* and in the Top 10 by *Bloomberg BusinessWeek*, CCL has offices in Greensboro, NC; Colorado Springs, CO; San Diego, CA; Brussels, Belgium; Moscow, Russia; Addis Ababa, Ethiopia; Johannesburg, South Africa; Singapore; Gurgaon, India; and Shanghai, China.

Ordering Information

To get more information, to order other books in the Ideas Into Action Series, or to find out about bulk-order discounts, please contact us by phone at 336-545-2810 or visit our online bookstore at www.ccl.org/Leadership/books.

CPSIA information can be obtained
at www.ICGtesting.com
Printed in the USA
LVOW01s1445240916

506054LV00038B/233/P